SPANISH BILINGUAL EDITION

Daycare Centre

by
Linda Kita-Bradley

Grass Roots Press

Copyright © 2016 Grass Roots Press

All rights reserved. No part of this book may be reproduced or transmitted in any form or by any means, including photocopy, recording, or any information storage and retrieval system, without the prior written permission of the publisher.

Daycare Centre is published by Grass Roots Press.
www.grassrootsbooks.net

ACKNOWLEDGMENTS

We acknowledge the financial support of the Government of Canada through the Canada Book Fund (CBF) for our publishing activities.

Produced with the assistance of the Government of Alberta, Alberta Multimedia Development Fund.

Translator: Sandra Gaviria-Buck
Photography: Grass Roots Press; Pages 4, 5, 6, 7: © BigStockPhoto

Library and Archives Canada Cataloguing in Publication

Kita-Bradley, Linda, 1958-, author
    Daycare centre / by Linda Kita-Bradley = La guardería / por Linda Kita-Bradley. -- Bilingual Spanish edition = Edición bilingüe español.

Titles from separate title pages;
Text in English with parallel Spanish translation.
ISBN 978-1-77153-114-6 (paperback)

    1. Readers for new literates. 2. Readers--Volunteers. 3. Readers--Voluntarism. 4. Readers--Day care centers. I. Kita-Bradley, Linda, 1958- . Daycare centre. II. Kita-Bradley, Linda, 1958- . Daycare centre. Spanish. III. Title. IV. Title: Guardería.

PE1126.N43K58253318 2016   428.6'2   C2016-903054-7

This is Val.

Val loves children.

Val wants a job in child care.

That means going back to school.

School means time.

School means money.

Val starts to save her money.

And she volunteers at a daycare centre.

This is Beth.

Beth works at the daycare.

Val helps Beth.

Val works with each child.

This child is sad.

Val talks with her.

This child is shy.
Val plays with her.

Val helps with lunch.

The children wash their hands.

The children eat lunch.

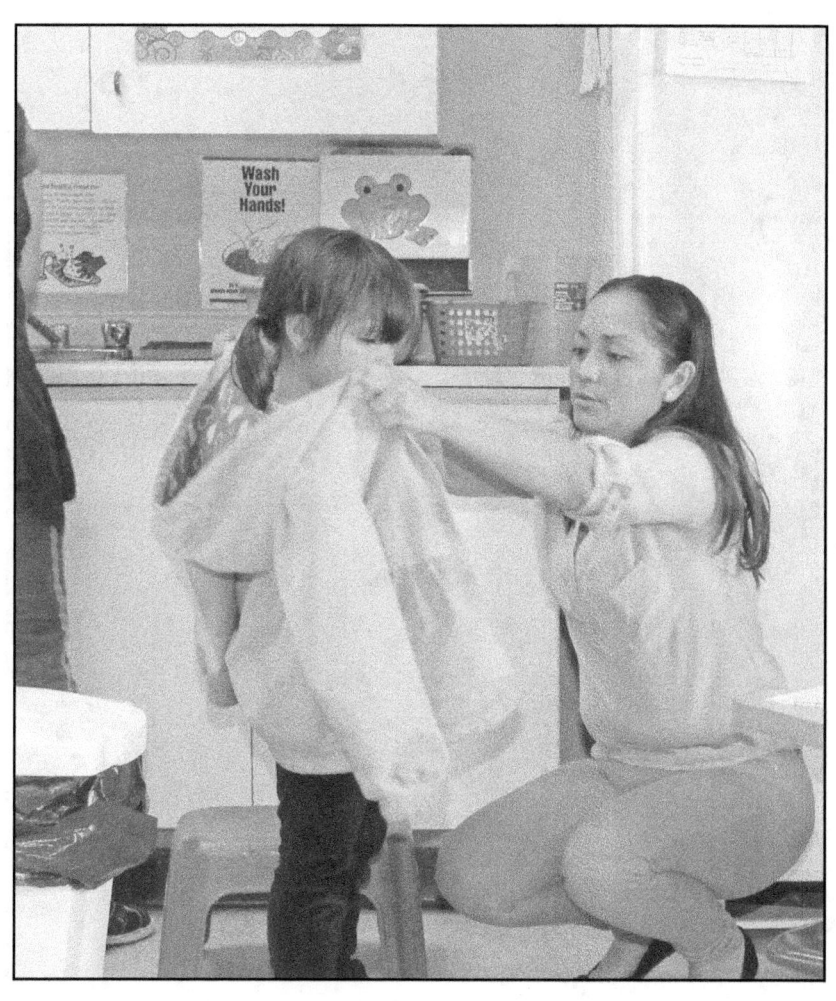

Then Val helps the children dress.

They go for a walk.

They go to the playground.

Finally, Val takes a break.

Beth asks, "How was your day?"

They plan the next day.

Val thinks, "Now I know for sure."

"I want a job in child care."

This is Val. Val loves children.
Val wants a job in child care.
That means going back to school.
School means time.
School means money.
Val starts to save her money.
And she volunteers at a daycare centre.
This is Beth.
Beth works at the daycare.
Val helps Beth.
Val works with each child.
This child is sad. Val talks with her.
This child is shy. Val plays with her.
Val helps with lunch.
The children wash their hands.
The children eat lunch.
Then Val helps the children dress.
They go for a walk.
They go to the playground.
Finally, Val takes a break.
Beth asks, "How was your day?"
They plan the next day.
Val thinks, "Now I know for sure."
"I want a job in child care."

Esta es Val. Val adora los niños.
Val quiere trabajar cuidando niños.
Para eso tiene que tomar unos cursos.
Volver a la escuela implica tiempo.
Volver a la escuela implica dinero.
Val comienza a ahorrar su dinero.
Y Val trabaja como voluntaria en una guardería.
Esta es Beth.
Beth trabaja en la guardería.
Val ayuda a Beth.
Val trabaja con cada niño.
Esta niña está triste. Val habla con ella.
Esta niña es tímida. Val juega con ella.
Val ayuda con el almuerzo.
Los niños se lavan las manos.
Los niños comen el almuerzo.
Luego Val ayuda a vestir los niños.
Salen a caminar.
Van al parque infantil.
Por fin, Val toma un descanso.
Beth pregunta, "¿Cómo estuvo tu día?"
Ellas planean el día siguiente.
Val piensa, "Ahora estoy segura."
"Quiero trabajar cuidando niños."

EDICIÓN BILINGÜE ESPAÑOL

La guardería

por
Linda Kita-Bradley

Grass Roots Press

Esta es Val.

Val adora los niños.

Val quiere trabajar cuidando niños.

Para eso tiene que tomar unos cursos.

Volver a la escuela implica tiempo.

Volver a la escuela implica dinero.
Val comienza a ahorrar su dinero.

Y Val trabaja como voluntaria en una guardería.

Esta es Beth.

Beth trabaja en la guardería.

Val ayuda a Beth

Val trabaja con cada niño.

Esta niña está triste.

Val habla con ella.

Esta niña es tímida.

Val juega con ella.

Val ayuda con el almuerzo.

Los niños se lavan las manos.

Los niños comen el almuerzo.

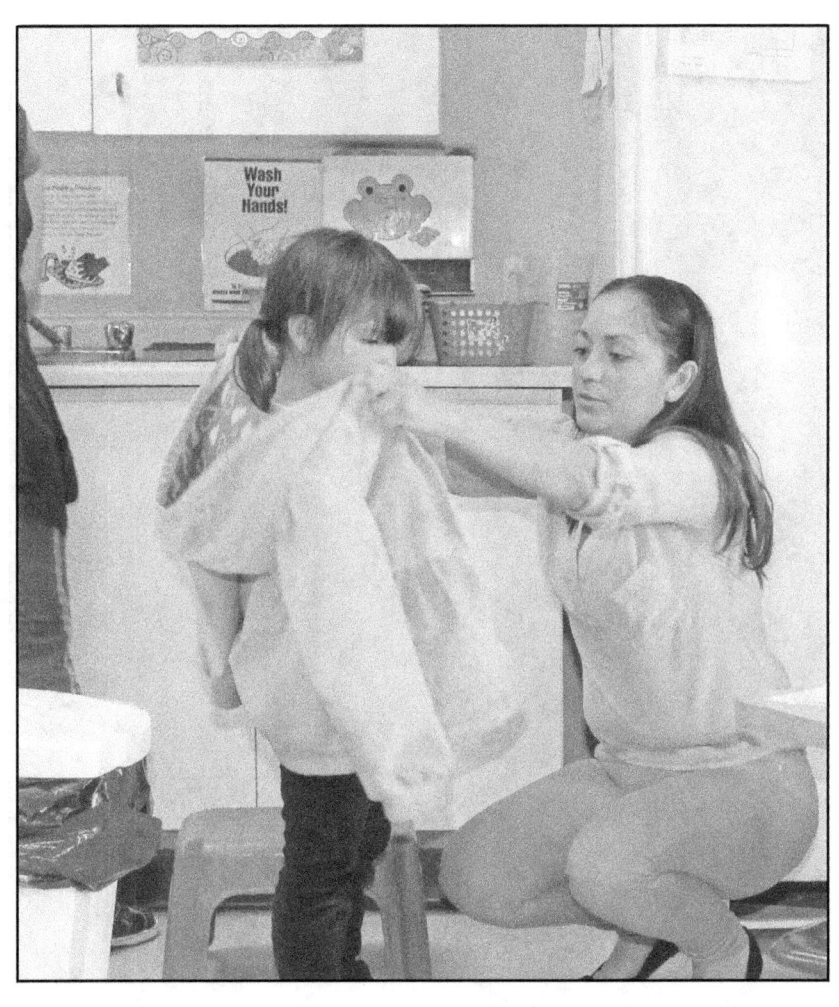

Luego Val ayuda a vestir los niños.

Salen a caminar.

Van al parque infantil.

Por fin, Val toma un descanso.

Beth pregunta, "¿Cómo estuvo tu día?"

Ellas planean el día siguiente.

Val piensa, "Ahora estoy segura."

"Quiero trabajar cuidando niños."

www.ingramcontent.com/pod-product-compliance
Lightning Source LLC
LaVergne TN
LVHW020940090426
835512LV00020B/3439